Living with dying

the management of terminal disease

DAME CICELY SAUNDERS
Medical Director, St. Christopher's Hospice
Sydenham, Kent

and

MARY BAINES
Physician, St. Christopher's Hospice,
Sydenham, Kent

OXFORD
OXFORD UNIVERSITY PRESS
NEW YORK   TORONTO
1983

Oxford University Press, Walton Street, Oxford OX2 6DP
London Glasgow New York Toronto
Delhi Bombay Calcutta Madras Karachi
Kuala Lumpur Singapore Hong Kong Tokyo
Nairobi Dar es Salaam Cape Town
Melbourne Auckland
and associate companies in
Beirut Berlin Ibadan Mexico City Nicosia

British Library Cataloguing in Publication Data

Saunders, Cicely
    Living with dying.—(Oxford medical publications)
    1. Death—Psychological aspects—Case studies
    2. Terminally ill—Psychology—Case studies
    I. Title   II. Baines, Mary
    362.1´75´0926   BF789.D4

ISBN 0-19-261404-5

Phototypeset by Cotswold Typesetting Ltd, Gloucester
Printed in Hong Kong

PREFACE

'It does not require a million pounds, or magic, but confidence that pain control is possible with detailed attention to a variety of therapeutic measures coupled with that attitude which accepts the whole patient and his needs but sees him as a person' (Ford and Pincherle 1978).

We believe that the suggestions in this book can be applied wherever a doctor finds that his commitment to his patient now includes treatment for terminal distress. They do not presuppose that the patient should be in a special hospice unit, though this move may have to be made to solve complex physical and social problems. These are basic principles that can be interpreted and developed anywhere and a special unit may never be needed.

Over the past two decades increasing attention has been given to the needs of dying patients and their families and the Hospice Movement has developed in diverse ways (Saunders et al. 1980). When St. Christopher's Hospice opened in 1967 as the first research and teaching hospice its main aim was that tested knowledge should flow back into all branches of the National Health Service, as well as to the older homes and hospices to which it owed so great a debt. That there should now be specialist wards in general hospitals and home and hospital teams working in consultation with the patient's own doctors are in many ways more important developments than the growth of special units. Most important of all has been the general change of attitude to a more analytical and positive approach to the needs of a dying patient and his family. Anecdotal evidence is replaced increasingly by objective data as the scientific foundations of this branch of medicine are laid. The essentials of good terminal management have been clarified and are now being widely discussed. Advances in this area of treatment (and it is still 'treatment', not some kind of soft option labelled 'care') are now likely to come from the traditional hospital setting as well as from the special units or teams. A patient, wherever he may be, should expect the same analytical attention to terminal suffering as he received for the original diagnosis and treatment of his condition. The aim is no longer cure but the chance of living to his fullest potential in physical ease and activity and with the assurance of personal relationships until he dies.

The achievement we will be looking for will be the patient's own. It is an honour as well as an education to meet people making their way through such adversity with the courage and common sense they so often show. We may see this only as we come near to them and we have often found that the best way is to develop skill in giving physical relief. We will not halt there if our patients give us the privilege of sharing their inner anguish. We may be able to do little to remove this but at the least we can stand by them. Our hope is that this book will make it easier to do so.

Sydenham   CS
April 1982   MJB

CONTENTS

1 INTRODUCTION

'I conceive it the office of the physician not only to restore the health but to mitigate pains and dolours; and not only when such mitigation may conduce to recovery but when it may serve to make a fair and easy passage.'

(Francis Bacon)

Health is more than the absence of disease or infirmity, it is the most effective use by an individual of his potential for living in physical, mental and social well-being (World Health Organization). The aim of the treatment of terminal disease is more than the mere absence of symptoms, it is that the patient and his family should live to the limits of their potential. The achievements to be looked for are not merely in physical ease and improvement, though these may be considerable, but in the use made of time given by these to deal with past problems, enjoy present opportunities, and probe future plans for the family who must live on afterwards (Earnshaw-Smith 1980): 'Terminal care refers to the management of patients in whom the advent of death is felt to be certain and not too far off and for whom medical effort has turned away from (active) therapy and become concentrated on the relief of symptoms and the support of both patient and family' (Holford 1973; slightly adapted). Many diseases have a terminal phase and patients suffering from them need treatment suited to their condition at that time. Doctors, however, are often unwilling to make such a judgement except in the various forms of malignant disease. These may have a comparatively long terminal phase, needing much skill and support if relief is to be given. Like most discussions on terminal care this book is concerned with malignant disease

but many of the symptoms to be treated and much of the
general management will be relevant to other situations.
What is being researched and taught in the hospices and
continuing care units is gradually spreading widely in the
general field. Terminal care should not only be a facet of
oncology but of geriatric medicine, neurology, general
practice, and throughout medicine.

On making decisions

A patient needs appropriate treatment at all stages of his
illness. When it is appreciated that palliative and terminal
care entail skilful and effective treatment and that the
direction is not only one way, doctors find it less difficult to
discontinue active therapy. Palliative care to combat persistent disease is often rigorous but it may give good returns in
active living or make curative treatment possible once again.
If it is no longer effective the alternative is not merely
custodial care; during the past decade or so it has become
clear that to practise competent terminal medicine is both
demanding and rewarding. It may give not only added
quality to the life remaining but also at times add con-
siderably to its length. For example, during the first 14 years
of St. Christopher's practice thirty two of the 1179 patients
who were admitted for terminal care for cancer of the breast
with widespread metastases have enjoyed lives of good
quality at home for *1–6 years* after their presenting symptoms
had been controlled while thirty one lived between six
months and a year. Their further care was shared between the
original treating hospital and the hospice wherever this was
appropriate. Symptom control alone or further radiotherapy,
chemotherapy, or hormone therapy made this possible.

Doctors are committed to giving appropriate care to their
patients, not to every treatment that may be technically
possible: 'The prolongation of life should not in itself

constitute the exclusive aim of medical practice, which must be concerned equally with the relief of suffering' (Council of Europe 1976).

These two aims must be balanced as the physician aims to act in the best interests of each patient. Ethical dilemmas are usually most satisfactorily considered in the context of particular situations (Lo and Johnson 1980). The risks, pain, likelihood of success, anticipated results, and side-effects are assessed for each patient. Not only physical but psychological and social aspects have to be considered and there must be opportunity to discuss the complex issues raised with all the staff involved. Although at times a 'trial of treatment', such as high-dose steroids for a patient with cerebral metastases (*see* p.37) is indicated it should be remembered that it is easier to withold possible treatments than it is to withdraw them once they have been instituted. The patient (if possible) and his family should still maintain their right to choose or refuse particular courses of action and a conference with all those involved, together with some of the professional team, may help greatly in giving accurate information and clarifying the issues. The use of the words 'ordinary' and 'extraordinary means', with the understanding that neither doctor nor patient need be committed to the latter (Pius XII 1957), does not excuse the doctor from going through an often complex process of deliberation to find what exactly they should mean for an individual patient. It has been suggested that when the actual criteria of decisions are specified the use of these words becomes redundant and may be omitted (*Journal of Medical Ethics* 1981).

A patient has a right to refuse treatment and to have his choice respected, provided he is mature and lucid. If he is unconscious, a document drawn up previously giving his general wishes may give the clinician some guidance as he makes his judgement. The relatives of a patient have no right to make decisions on his behalf unless he is incompetent. They may act only in his best interests and should be helped to consider what these are by discussion with the different members of the professional team.

The doctor may not embark on any conduct with the primary intention of causing the patient's death and if a terminally ill patient expresses a desire to commit suicide a doctor may not in law facilitate the suicide (Suicide Act 1961). To do so would be a criminal offence (Kennedy 1978). He cannot respond to similar suggestions by the family to act deliberately to end life. Effective therapy and adequate explanations should dispel the misunderstandings fairly widespread among the public that doctors are committed to prolonging life whatever its quality and that the only way to a peaceful dying is by a deliberate overdose. To ease the pains of death has always been one of the commitments of medical practice and if, to ease suffering, a doctor must take measures which may hasten death, this is permissible provided that the doctor's aim is only the relief of pain or other distress. This reflects the so-called double effect theory and was incorporated into English law in one of the few decided cases in this area (Rex *v*. Bodkin Adams 1957).

The overlapping of the arrows in Fig. 1 indicates that skilled control of the problems of advanced and terminal disease does not necessarily have to wait until all other treatment is abandoned; its successful use may indeed make that treatment more effective. When the clinician is involved with both chemotherapy *and* with the control of pain and

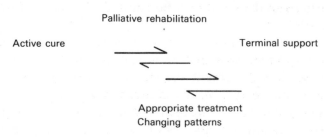

Fig. 1.

nausea, it will be easier to recognize diminishing returns to the former and to discontinue it without any member of the team or of the family feeling that now *no* treatment is being given. To accept a situation when treatment is directed to the relief of symptoms and the alleviation of general distress will no longer mean an implicit 'there is nothing more that we can do' but an explicit 'everything possible is being done'. Our concern and interest in this field brings us to the dying person with ever-renewed concern and a positive attitude that is often transferred without words: 'It can do much to lift the feeling of helplessness from the situation and help the patient to die with a sense of worth to the end' (Vanderpool 1978). Nothing could undermine this more than any form of legalized deliberate ending of life. A 'right to die' could all too easily become a 'presumed duty to die' (Hansard 1976).

Vanderpool and others have come to consider that, although popular, the phrase 'death with dignity' is used with such different interpretations that it is better abandoned. It suffers from a dangerous ambiguity, and serves to mask three quite distinct demands:

1. That the individual should in principle be free to determine whether he shall live or die and that, in the event of his choosing to die, he should be entitled to be assisted in so doing by the medical profession, except in so far as his rights are limited in the general interest.

2. That a doctor should with the patient's consent be free, under certain safeguards, to end the patient's life in cases (if there are such) where it is medically impossible to control the pain.

3. That (i) a patient *in extremis* should not be subjected to troublesome treatments which cannot restore him to health; and (ii) doctors may use drugs to control pain even at the risk of shortening life.

(3) does not entail euthanasia at all, for it does not entail deliberately killing the patient. (1) entails euthanasia on a different basis from (2) and on a larger scale. An expression

which suffers from this degree of ambiguity is dangerously unsuitable for use in serious discussion (Church Information Office 1975). In its conclusion the Working Party stated, 'To justify a change in the law in this country to permit euthanasia, it would be necessary to show that such a change would remove greater evils than it would cause. We do not believe that such justification can be given' (Church Information Office 1975).

The question of truth

Those who are close to a patient with a terminal illness have to consider the questions, spoken and unspoken, that this person is asking. Over the past 20 years doctors in the UK have become more inclined to tell cancer patients the truth of their diagnosis (*Lancet* 1980) and to consider the demands made upon their time and understanding by the continuing communication that is needed if morale is to be sustained (Brewin 1977). A patient can hardly be expected to go through modern cancer management without being given some explanation and some control over what is being done to his disease and to his life, although the less traumatic words— e.g. 'tumour'—may be used. At the same time we have to consider how much we tell the family. We need to consider what we do to close relationships when totally different information is given. At times we may perhaps consider giving the family a rather less gloomy prognosis and the patient a somewhat more realistic picture and, as soon as possible, go on to talk with them together. We must not forget that the patient may well be the strongest member of the family, ill though he is. But whatever is said may have to be said repeatedly, for the many questions that need to be asked may emerge only gradually.

Feelings of helplessness and hopelessness and unquestioning acceptance have been shown to have adverse effects upon prognosis (Greer *et al.* 1979). These can only be exacerbated by poor rapport, silence, and evasions. The feeling of isolation that these engender undermines all morale. There are undoubtedly some patients who do not wish to face truth and who will continue to push it out of their minds. Denial, as well as a fighting spirit, were both shown to correlate with recurrence-free survival (Greer *et al*. 1979) and whatever we do or say, many patients are able to maintain this as their choice in the matter. Aitken-Swan and Easson (1959) reported follow-up inverviews with 231 patients who had been told their diagnosis, reassured that the disease was early, and told that treatment should cure them. They found that two-thirds of the patients were glad to have known the truth, 7 per cent resented the consultant's frankness, and 19 per cent denied that they had been told at all (Aitken-Swan and Easson 1959). At St. Christopher's Hospice we found during 1977 that nearly 22 per cent of these patients referred from hospital who were reported to have had their diagnosis and/or prognosis fully explained to them had apparently no knowledge of this when they talked to the hospice doctors; 13.5 per cent of those referred by their family doctors with the same report appeared to have no insight (West and Kirkham 1980).

It has been suggested that patients referred to a hospice must surely have full insight into their diagnosis and likely prognosis. A recent hospice survey of 100 patients carried out by a research nurse within 48 hours of admission showed that while approximately half the patients revealed that they knew their diagnosis only about one third were prepared at that time to admit to knowledge of their prognosis (Walsh and Bowman 1981). The doctors who saw these patients on admission did not always elicit the same answers. Experience suggests that at least some people find it easier to begin such discussions first with a nurse, someone who is not expected to make definite pronouncements, but the differences were not all of this nature.

Evidently while many are glad to have been given the opportunity to handle knowledge, failure either to absorb or to retain it still remains a possible choice, conscious or unconscious. But we must be ready for changes in our patients' knowledge and attitude. During the course of a deteriorating illness truth is likely to seep gradually into the consciousness of most patients. It happens as they watch and listen to other patients, as they remember previous illness and deceptions in the family, and as they notice the avoidances and evasions of those around them. Sometimes there is the more dramatic sighting of notes, the blood request form or the like. If honest discussion has already been put out of court, how much support and reassurance can then be given? Many of the patients of the studies quoted above moved into more open discussions and fuller insight during their stay in the hospice. This has often helped families to draw together to face their mutual loss.

To be told of a threatening diagnosis at the stage when treatment with hopes of a cure can be offered is hardly the same as a discussion of the disease when it has reached its terminal stage. Yet the earlier policy of at least a guarded truth will make it easier for both patient and doctor to adjust to the new conditions. The patient is then more ready to believe it when he is told that symptoms can be controlled and that any crisis will be dealt with: 'Implicit in the doctor–patient relationship is that the patient will not be abandoned if things go wrong' (*Lancet* 1980).

When things are not going well, for each patient there will be different answers to the question, 'how much should the truth be discussed, at what stage, and with whom?' Those doctors who advocate a greater degree of openness concerning diagnosis during the early stages may wish to continue their optimisms, even if more cautiously, to the end. Some patients are glad to go along with this. McIntosh found that such a practice seemed to work well in the wards he studied in a year's participant observation and he believed that it was approved by most patients (McIntosh 1978). Others have found that daily small reassurances will carry many people through until almost the end of their lives so long as the staff helping them will tackle each practical problem as it arises (Graeme 1961). We believe that when time is available for unhurried discussion most people are glad of the opportunity to express their deeper fears but they may need our help in initiating such discussions. They feel themselves at a disadvantage when faced with the doctor's greater knowledge and tendency to speak from a height (Holden 1980). Many people need greatly to talk about their deteriorating condition with someone who is concerned and who is also confident that this part of life is important and that when symptoms are controlled it can still be lived creatively. Such discussion may take several brief sessions and are often interspersed with apparently contradictory optimism. But all of us spend time reading holiday brochures and complicated menus that we know we will never undertake.

Those who continue to use denial to the end in order to protect themselves should not be assaulted by truths that they are neither willing nor able to handle. Some of them will do well, living from day to day, and their families are likely to go along with their lack of realism, often with considerable relief. Their choice is to be respected and seems to be the usual approach in a number of countries where this topic has been discussed.

There is evidence that in the UK a more open approach is appreciated as a patient nears death. Hinton (1963) carried out a controlled study of a group of dying patients in the wards of a London teaching hospital. The results showed that 50 per cent of his 102 dying patients already had a shrewd idea of the severity of their illness when he first interviewed them and that 'awareness of dying grew so that three out of every four spoke of this possibility or certainty'. These patients had often not been 'told' and the ward staff were often unaware that they had such knowledge. Later he studied eighty patients dying in four different settings; two where the policy was to avoid any discussion of unpalatable truth and two

which encouraged attempts at more honest communication.
The last two groups were less anxious and depressed and
welcomed the greater openness (Hinton 1979). Although, as
he points out, no general principle can tell us what we must
say to an individual patient it can give us guide lines and
encourage us not to take automatically the easy path of
evasions.

All of us have to listen with care and respond to what we
hear, however inexperienced we may feel. It is possible to
learn to assess a patient's readiness or otherwise to assimilate
bad news. Clues are given as we listen to questions and to
silences and observe a patient's choice of time and listener for
his comments and queries. However experienced we may be
we do not have a technique to offer to others for their
emulation, only some confidence in a patient's courage and
common sense to hand on to the newcomer in this field.
Communication takes place on many levels but once a patient
understands that he will get a considered answer to any
question he may gradually become ready to face his situation
more fully. Even then it may take several visits from the
doctor and much discussion with the ward team. We can deal
with a person honestly without moving directly into stark
truth. We have to try to face openly what he wants to reveal of
his thoughts and try to meet him where he is, making as it
were an alliance with him. As Parkes suggests, 'He may say,
"I am frightened of dying", and we may hastily murmur,
"Yes, of course", and change to some more cheerful subject.
Yet the dying patient may fear many things and a more
appropriate response may be, "Are you? Well tell me just
what you mean by that." Encouraged to talk further, the
patient will then express fears, some of which may be quite
needless' (Parkes 1978a).

Much discussion with the patient will continue to take
place in the context of symptom analysis and control and
when they feel free to express unrealistic fears we can provide
reassurance. When they can share with us their realistic

apprehensions concerning dependence and loss we can help them to express the grief they feel at their own weakness and the partings that loom ahead. We will often be impressed by their courage and their common sense. When we have been honest in the past our reassurances that pain will not be allowed to escape control and that death itself will be peaceful are more likely to be accepted (*see* Mental Pain, p.53).

2 TERMINAL PAIN

The greatest fear of all is the fear of pain and all too often this fear has been justified. Terminal pain is often treated ineptly and the view of the public that death from cancer is likely to be accompanied by unremitting distress continues to be confirmed. The vast majority of these patients (and many of those with other diseases) could be given good relief by the competent use of narcotic analgesics and their adjuvants. Such treatment is denied them because of misconceptions concerning the use and effectiveness of these drugs; yet experience in many countries during the past two decades has shown that terminal pain can be thus relieved often over long periods without impairment of the patient's alertness or personality and that they can be withdrawn if no longer needed. An adequate analysis of the sometimes complex causes of terminal distress will lead to appropriate treatment, in some cases with specific measures such as radiotherapy, chemotherapy, and nerve blocks but for most patients by the right use of the pharmacology now available which, used as part of a general approach, will maintain quality of life to the end.

Its nature

A series of pictures painted by St. Christopher's patients illustrated how they saw the pain with which they presented. The feeling of being impaled by a red-hot nail, of being totally isolated from the world by the encircling 'muscles of tension' with nothing but a hypodermic to pierce through them, the sudden jabs on movement, and the implacable heaviness of pain were all illustrated vividly. So too was the

Fig. 2. A patient (Mrs E.S.) draws the feeling of being constantly at the mercy of some kind of demolition squad.

conviction that one is no better than some kind of scrap heap or exists at the mercy of the demolition squad, suffering blow after blow (Fig. 2).

These paintings express feelings that are common to many patients dying of cancer. The somewhat artificial division of such pain into separate components helps the therapist to decide whether his assessment is adequate. Patients use such phrases as 'It was *all* pain', 'The pain was all around me', and 'You can't think about anything else'. It is no exaggeration to term such suffering 'Total Pain' and it may help to divide it into physical, emotional, social, and spiritual components. The pain which causes an animal to remain motionless while an injured part heals is a total 'feeling state'. Wall suggests that pain is better classified as a need state than as a sensation, serving more to promote healing than to avoid injury (Wall 1979). Terminal pain is certainly a need state but it rarely promotes healing and has no such built-in meaning for those who suffer it. Rather it traps the patient in a situation for which there is no comforting explanation and to which there is no foreseeable end. This is a radically different pain from the postoperative pain which has been researched by many workers from Beecher (1960) onwards and which forms a large part of teaching-hospital experience. Such pain is easily understood by the patient and we can ask considerable endurance of people who can expect recovery and who are coming through an event limited in time. Pain as a protective reflex is equally purposeful and comprehensible.

A few patients have suffered so greatly from 'total pain' before admission to the Hospice that they have attempted suicide. More might well have taken this step were they not convinced that this would be especially hurtful to their families, adding feelings of guilt and rejection to the losses of bereavement.

Case history

Mr H. G., aged 73, had surgery for a carcinoma of stomach, followed over the next months by six courses of chemotherapy. He developed severe pain which was not relieved in spite of increasing doses of analgesics until in June 1978 he twice attempted to kill himself, first with an overdose of dextromoramide, which by this time he was taking hourly, and later by slashing his wrists. On transfer to the Hospice he said 'The pain was driving me crazy'.

His pain was controlled within 48 hours by oral morphine, which was given four hourly. His comment after 12 hours was, 'Last night's sleep was a gift'. The dose was increased in the following 3 weeks from 30–60 mg and chlorpromazine 25–50 mg was used as an adjuvant. As soon as he was free of pain he no longer wished to end his life but as the disease progressed he became increasing weak and dyspnoeic. During his last few days he had occasional episodes of confusion but he was still able to walk to the toilet the day before he died.

A determined clarification of the responsibility for symptom control between the family doctor and the two hospitals involved and its vigorous pursuit at the time Mr H. G. was still being given chemotherapy should have been able to relieve a pain which the hospice did not find difficult to control. He should have had such relief for the full 9 months of his advancing illness and not merely during the final 3 weeks. Referral to a pain clinic for consideration of a coeliac axis block might have been considered at an earlier stage but oral morphine given regularly with continual dose assessment and diamorphine given intramuscularly during his last 24 hours were sufficient to control his pain without impairment of his affect or alertness.

Incidence

Parkes' study, from which Fig. 3 is taken, was carried out during 1967–72. It showed that among 276 married patients under the age of 65 who died of cancer in two London Boroughs, forty nine were still under active treatment at the time of death and that while the length of time after the end of such treatment varied greatly, the median length of terminal care was 9 weeks. Parkes divided these patients into *home*

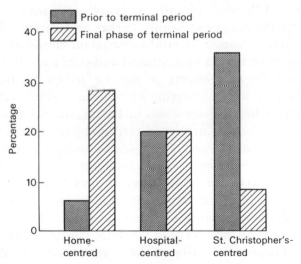

Fig. 3. Proportions of patients with severe and mostly continuous pain (*Dr Colin Murray Parkes, with permission*).

based, including in this group all who died within a week of a final hospital admission; *hospital based;* and *St. Christopher's based*. The amount of pre-terminal and terminal pain reported by their next-of-kin afterwards is shown in Fig. 3 (Parkes 1978b). This study was repeated 10 years later as part of the evaluation of the work of the hospice and initial analysis shows improvement in all settings.

Not only are patients who died in 1977–9 said (by their spouses) to have suffered much less pain during the terminal period in hospital or hospice than those who died in 1967–9, but they are also said to have suffered less pain prior to the end of active treatment and during any period of care at home. Corresponding improvements in the amount of distress suffered by patients and by spouses were also reported during this decade.

Although improvements in pain relief mean that pain is no longer a major difficulty in either hospice or hospital, it can still be a problem at home. Twenty-one per cent are said to have suffered severe pain at home and 46 per cent of the spouses had themselves suffered 'very great anxiety' while caring for the patient at home (Parkes and Parkes 1982).

Although retrospective studies based on family memories are likely to be biased by confused and confusing feelings— such as guilt at allowing a patient to go to hospital, rationalization at not bringing him home, and projection of the angry feelings so common in bereavement—Woodbine (1977) showed that unrelieved terminal pain is still all too common. He interviewed ninety-seven patients identified by their doctors as dying of their malignancy, sixty-three at home and thirty-four in hospital. Thirty-four per cent of both groups reported moderate or severe pain in the 24 hours before interview, despite a variety of drugs. He comments that the medications written up only rarely included the narcotic analgesics and that of the twenty-nine patients with pain only four 'received strong pain drugs on the day of interview'.

Another paper has shown how much pain goes unrecog-
nized in a general teaching hospital where 'nurses accept the
presence of unrelieved pain in patients too readily, as
indicated by the practice of confining enquiry about pain to
drug rounds and by ignoring non-verbal communication'
(Hunt *et al.* 1977).

Analysis

It is revealing to find how many patients with terminal
disease are surprised to find a doctor who will listen to the
story of their suffering. While they appreciated the care and
concern that have been focused on the signs of their disease
they often say that it is the first time that anyone has paid
attention to the most troublesome aspects of it. As we listen to
each patient and to his family we are assessing the nature of
the pain on the physical level, identifying its nature, sites and
possible causes but also assessing its implications for him,
with his family background and culture, past experience, and
present anxieties.

An analysis of past history, accurate elucidation of present
symptoms, a competent and thorough clinical examination
and appropriate investigations are still demanded at this stage
of the disease. It is not, as before, to make a diagnosis of the
nature of the disease but rather to diagnose the causes of the
symptoms produced by the now incurable disease. Once we
know why a patient has pain or vomiting, is breathless or
confused, we can give him more effective treatment for his
distress. Terminal suffering should be approached as an
illness in itself, one that will respond to rationally based
treatment.

Baines' study analyses the causes of pain in the first 100
patients with malignant disease admitted to St. Christopher's
Hospice in 1980. Of these 100 patients, eighty-two were in
pain and eighteen were without pain. The details are shown
in Table 1. There were 114 separate causes of pain in eighty-

TABLE 1 *Causes of pain in the first* 100 *patients with malignant disease admitted to St. Christopher's Hospice in 1980*

Visceral pain	29	Lymphoedema	3
Bone pain	17	Headaches due to ICP	3
Soft-tissue infiltration	10	Pain in paralysed limb(s)	3
Nerve compression	9	Generalized aches	3
Secondary infection	6	Non-malignant causes	17
Pleural pain	4	Cause unknown	6
Colic due to obstruction	4		

two patients. In no case was the cause thought to be purely psychogenic, though it was realized that depression and anxiety and family, financial and spiritual problems often lower the thresholds for pain and thus increase the total pain experience.

Referral to other disciplines

The radiotherapy and oncology departments and the pain clinic are likely to be called on most often, although the help of most of the specialities of a general hospital may be needed from time to time.

Palliative radiotherapy may be helpful during the last weeks of a patient's life, provided it is applied skilfully. It must be given without delay, with the minimum number of treatments, and its benefit must have been carefully balanced against the price the patient has to pay in terms of the time and trouble entailed. Its aim is to relieve symptoms with the lowest possible dose in the fewest possible treatments and with the minimum side-effects. It may have an important part to play in the relief of pain from bone metastases and for many sites may be given on the day the patient is first seen in the department so that only one visit is necessary. Pelvic and vertebral metastases will need a fractionated course of treatment. The bone and joint pains of patients in the late stages of leukaemia respond to irradiation and the painful joints of hypertrophic pulmonary osteoarthropathy may be relieved by treating a primary bronchial carcinoma. Irradiation of a collapsing cervical or dorsal vertebra should be considered as a prophylatic measure against possible incontinence and paralysis. A collapse causing paralysis is an emergency calling for immediate treatment or decompression if the patient's condition warrants this. Nerve-root pain due to vertebral collapse and the severe pain of nerve plexus involvement is difficult to control by radiotherapy; this is a place for nerve-blocking procedures although analgesics and high-dose cortiosteroids may also be used with benefit.

Radiotherapy may also be considered for the relief of haemoptysis, haematuria, or vaginal bleeding, all of which are very disturbing to the patient and the family. It may be used to control fungation and discharge and to relieve cough and dyspnoea by treating either the primary tumour or mediastinal and other lymph nodes (Bates 1978).

Regular rounds with a radiotherapist/oncologist are essential for a hospice or continuing care unit, not only to discuss the patients selected by the terminal care team but also to review others who could benefit from these two disciplines. Such rounds have taken place regularly over the past years at St. Christopher's Hospice. Initially, they identified some 5–10 per cent of the total patient population as still likely to benefit. These patients are now often discussed by telephone with the radiotherapist/oncologist and this liaison is as straightforward as that of a continuing care unit which is part of the general hospital. Modified chemotherapeutic regimens and hormone manipulation have become part of hospice practice.

A similar exercise has recently been carried out in developing a closer link with a pain clinic. During the past 3 years regular rounds which reviewed all patients in the sixty-two hospice beds have been organized. As the Hospice patients have a median stay of 13–14 days many patients were too ill to be considered but some 5 per cent were thought likely to benefit. Various procedures have been carried out on most of these patients (forty in 1979, sixty in 1980 and over sixty in 1981), the majority with good, lasting relief. Such co-operation between pain clinics and hospices is necessary and increasing.

3 THE USE OF ANALGESICS FOR TERMINAL PAIN

While there is no need to resort automatically to strong analgesics when a patient approaches the terminal stages of his illness, pain must be relieved as soon as it becomes a matter for complaint. We may have to elicit such complaint, for these patients often underestimate our interest in their pain or the possibility of relief.

The essential first step is the careful taking of the history, which is a prerequisite of all effective work in this field and a therapeutic tool in itself. Adequate relief must be given from the beginning of the patient's downhill course for he should become accustomed to expect freedom from discomfort rather than its constant presence. The effect of pain is greatly influenced by past experience of pain and in turn it creates the expectation of future pain. If fear is aroused it will immediately enhance pain by tension and once it has become established pain is likely to need larger doses for its relief. The dramatic ease that may be given by an *injection* naturally enhances any tendency to rely upon drugs. Crises should be anticipated and prevented wherever possible; injections should rarely be needed.

Mild pain

The relief of mild terminal pain can usually be achieved with weak analgesics, which may be sufficient throughout an entire illness. A well-tried remedy in which a patient has built up confidence over the months may also be used later as a standby to supplement more powerful medication.

Aspirin and the newer non-steroidal anti-inflammatory

drugs have long been used for all types of bone and joint pain in terminal disease. The work that has clarified the mechanisms of their action has endorsed years of trust in their effectiveness and in the view of many hospice doctors aspirin is still the most useful remedy for mild pain of all kinds in terminal illness. Its dangers are not great in proportion to the number of patients who will benefit and are acceptable in this situation. Although gastric upset is not uncommon it can usually be avoided by a sensible routine for taking medication, by trying different presentations of this valuable and versatile drug and by the use of antacids. It is important to discover a patient's preferences and idiosyncrasies.

There are other drugs for such pain. Despite recent evidence of its potential dangers, dextropropoxyphene, with or without paracetamol or aspirin (as Distalgesic, Doloxene or Darvon), continues to be widely used. It may benefit those patients who feel that aspirin is too 'ordinary' to be of help to them, and as these preparations need a doctor's prescription and come in unaccustomed forms and colours they may be expected to bring with them some placebo response. However, it is probably wise to find an alternative to the patient's taste.

We must be aware of the importance of factors other than pure drug action. Enthusiasm, careful instructions, and the doctor's own confidence often do more to relieve terminal pain than any drugs. It is because enthusiastic interest is so often denied to the patient with terminal cancer that his pain becomes so fraught with misery.

Moderate pain

Moderate pain may be relieved by one of a number of analgesics but alone and in combination codeine is a well-known standby and serves as a standard. There are a number of drugs that appear to be equianalgesic in studies but vary in their clinical effectiveness. Dihydrocodeine will help one patient and render another intractably constipated. Dipipanone (Diconal) is more powerful. It keeps some patients fully mobile while others are rendered so drowsy and lethargic (possible by the amount of cyclizine in each tablet) that they cannot take them at all. There is no evidence that dipipanone is any more nauseating than other analgesics but it is not obtainable alone. Mixed preparations are usually to be avoided. It is better to discover a patient's own best combination of drugs.

In our view there is little place for the use of pentazocine or pethidine in terminal care. Neither are potent oral analgesics and both are comparatively short acting. Pentazocine has the additional drawback of an unacceptably high proportion of patients experiencing psychotomimetic side-effects. Dextromoramide is more potent but is relatively short acting and a considerable number of patients have been admitted to St. Christopher's taking this drug two or even one hourly. It is useful, however, as a cover for a painful episode when given as a supplement to other regular medication. Papaveretum and opium are often combined with aspirin and are given for moderate pain, often over long periods, in radiotherapy departments and some of the hospices. They may be the only oral opiates available in some countries. Oral morphine and diamorphine (such as 5–10 mg oral morphine) may be the most valuable of all drugs used to control moderate pain. They should usually be given on a 4 hourly routine at the dose needed to give uninterrupted relief. There is no constant pattern of dose increase and patients are often successfully maintained on the same dose for weeks or months. Nor is there any problem in reducing the dose or withdrawing the narcotic altogether if pain control is later achieved by other means.

Sustained-release morphine sulphate (MST-1 Continus, 10 mg) has recently become available. Pharmacological studies have shown that blood concentrations of morphine remain raised for 12 hours after administration and yet there is an absence of accumulation of the drug with repeated therapy. Clinical experience has confirmed the usefulness of the preparation in moderate pain. It is given 12 hourly, usually starting with one tablet and increasing the dose as necessary. In practice we have found that if pain is not controlled with three or four tablets 12 hourly the patient should be transferred to morphine solution 4 hourly and the dose titrated against his requirements. However, high dose tablets are becoming available and for many patients a tablet taken twice daily is preferable to a mixture that has to be taken every 4 hours. We await further studies of this preparation.

Analgesics by suppository are valuable in home care. In our hands morphine by this route has not been as effective as oxycodone pectinate (Proladone). Used at 8 or sometimes 6 hourly intervals it may make home care a possibility for patients with severe pain who can take nothing by mouth. Chlorpromazine and prochlorperazine suppositories may be added for patients with nausea and/or vomiting and should be considered if a patient's injection sites become painful.

Severe pain

Case history

The wife of a patient with severe pain from far advanced cancer is told by the houseman that the opiates are 'dangerous drugs' and that he will become addicted if he is given them 'too soon'.

He is finally written up for injections of morphine but the doses are spaced out beyond the effectiveness of the dose selected and often arrive late so that he is constantly in pain and waiting for relief. He is always anxious. A decision to try an oral mixture is made on a Friday, the dose given is ineffective and the houseman does not know what to do as no instructions have been left. The patient has a miserable weekend with greatly increased pain. Near the end of his life he is still anxiously clock-watching as he waits for the next injection. At this point they are altered and become heavily sedative and he never speaks again clearly to his wife, who, like him, had been told till then that there were weeks or months ahead.

Similar stories continue to be repeated because misconceptions of the use of the strong analgesics deny relief to many patients. Fears of producing tolerance, psychological dependence, and respiratory depression are prevalent, repeated escalations of dose are anticipated, and both patients and doctors fear a time when nothing can be effective. It is though that there is no middle road between a patient in pain and one heavily sedated, and because no proper standard of pain relief with unaffected sensorium exists in the clinician's mind he accepts these alternatives as inevitable.

For many years those caring for large numbers of patients with severe terminal pain have believed that nothing could replace the opiates and have known that they could be given without such problems. Although new understanding of pain mechanisms and of its chemistry may alter our approach and give us new tools during the next decade patients need relief *now* and should expect the knowledge of how to give it to them from any doctor. No foreseeable number of hospices or pain clinics is going to reach the majority of the terminally ill who are at present suffering pain and other physical distress. Nor would it be right that such units or teams should undertake the care of all these patients as an exclusive speciality. Skill and confidence in handling analgesics and their adjuvants must become part of general medical education and whoever treats these patients must know when to begin with narcotic drugs, what routine to establish, and what other medications to combine with them.

When to begin

When terminal pain escapes control with moderate analgesics or when the patient finds he has to swallow more than two pills to obtain relief it is time for the smaller dose of a stronger drug. If a patient is already on small doses of a narcotic, an increase in pain should lead to an increase in dose but vigorous effort must be made again to identify the cause of the increased pain and consider any specific treatment that may be available and appropriate. The clinical team should be as ready to consider the various measures for pain control as to discuss different forms of active treatment and should record plans for pain relief in the notes. Any continuing problems must be reviewed constantly but there is no need to deny a patient relief of severe pain while its detailed aetiology is investigated. Adequate relief must be given as soon as possible and we believe that the drug of choice is still morphine, the most versatile and flexible available. If pain is relieved later by other means it can easily be discontinued, physical signs of withdrawal are rare and will be avoided by tapering the dose over several days. If this fact were more widely recognized this drug might less often be withheld from those with non-malignant terminal disease causing severe pain.

Routine for pain prevention

The typical pain of terminal cancer is constant in character, although it may have exacerbations such as on movement. Constant pain calls for constant control, not a desperate switch back between bouts of pain and periods of somnolent relief: 'In our hospital the patients *earn* their morphine' (a medical student). Pain itself is the strongest antagonist to the drugs given to suppress it and it is of cardinal importance that neither its presence nor its threat should act against relief. If a patient has to ask for his analgesic he will be reminded each time of his dependence on the drug and on the person who gives it to him. If it is given regularly with a slightly relaxed schedule so that no one is obsessively clock-watching and at a dose that covers the extra period of relief that may be required should a dose be delayed, then pain can be forgotten and the self-perpetuating spiral of misery and dependence is not initiated. Continual expectations of the recurrence of pain with p.r.n. narcotic orders is the route to iatrogenically induced dependence.

Vere's series of diagrams (Figs. 4–8) illustrate how the regular giving of narcotics by mouth prevents pain break-through by keeping the plasma drug concentration continuously in the patient's own effective zone and below the level of toxicity. Oral doses, yielding a more rounded peak than intravenous administration, facilitate this. Doses should be regularly spaced, including a night dose for most patients, who will prefer being woken for a dose rather than by pain some time later (Vere 1978). If injections are necessary because of vomiting or dysphagia a similar routine should be maintained. Slow-release morphine may of course make a night dose unnecessary.

Many years of experience have shown that tolerance is not a clinical problem and that when it occurs it has usually been induced by unnecessary, automatic dose increase. Should a patient's pain break through and he need a larger dose his effective zone has shifted and this is as true for respiratory

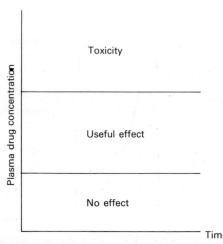

Fig. 4. Plasma concentration zones in relation to drug effects (*Vere (1978), with permission*).

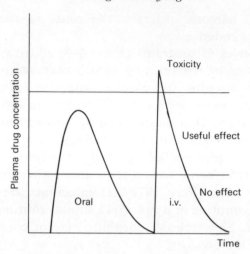

Fig. 5. Oral and intravenous plasma concentration-time curves (*Vere (1978), with permission*).

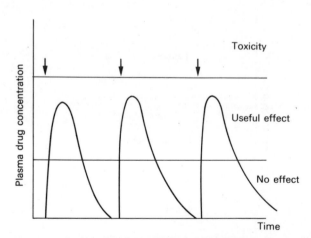

Fig. 6. Doses spaced too widely to maintain analgesia. Larger doses at the same frequency would only increase toxicity (*Vere (1978), with permission*).

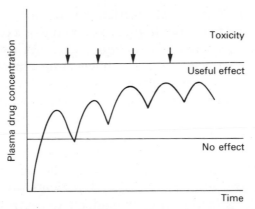

Fig. 7. Doses spaced at satisfactory intervals to maintain analgesia (*Vere (1978), with permission*).

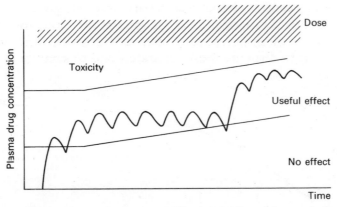

Fig. 8. The effects of tolerance (*Vere (1978), with permission*).

depression and other side-effects as for analgesia. In a recent series of twenty hospice patients on high-dose narcotics of whom several had pre-existing respiratory disease, nineteen were found to have pCo_2 values within normal limits.

Sequential increases in oral doses are usually in increments of 5 mg for doses of less than 20 mg, then to 30 mg, 45 mg, and 60 mg and thereafter each increase is usually in the range of 20–30 mg. The maximum effective oral dose is ill defined but in our practice doses higher than 90 mg or a reduction of the interval to 3 hourly are seldom needed. As Twycross has shown (Fig. 9) tolerance seems to level off in most cases and usually ceases to operate after a few weeks (Twycross 1978). Psychological dependence does not occur and whilst physical dependence may develop it does not prevent the downward adjustment of the dose of narcotic when considered clinically possible. Some hospices are now using automated narcotic administration in their wards and in the home and have reported excellent pain control with patients who presented with problems of vomiting or inadequate control. A reduction in the doses needed as well as a return to oral medication have been found possible and have enabled many patients to die comfortably in their own homes.

In many centres phenothiazines are routinely given with an oral narcotic solution, although it appears that their antiemetic effect is often not needed after 48–72 hours. The usual practice is to dispense these separately and to keep the doses

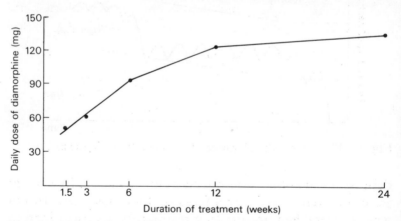

Fig. 9. 418 patients admitted consecutively with advanced cancer were grouped according to survival following the start of treatment with diamorphine; group median final daily dose of diamorphine is shown plotted again group median duration of treatment (*Twycross, with permission*).

relatively stable while altering the narcotic. It is the increase in drugs of the phenothiazine group that usually causes the over-sedation too often seen in general wards. Other adjuvant medication should also be added individually and only one drug change should be made at a time. A degree of polypharmacy is indicated for many of these patients but this must be carefully monitored and regularly reviewed.

Absorption of oral narcotics

Despite long-term effective use in various centres objections are still heard concerning the use of oral narcotics on the grounds of poor and unreliable absorption. On the basis of urinary excretion studies, Twycross *et al.* (1974) estimated that diamorphine is probably completely absorbed from the gastrointestinal tract and that morphine is some two-thirds absorbed.

A further study in which assay of serum 'morphine' equivalents was by radioimmunoassay. Venous blood from sixty-five patients receiving diamorphine hydrochloride and twenty-four receiving morphine sulphate showed a highly significant positive linear correlation between the dose administered and the serum concentration ($P < 0.001$) with respect to both drugs (Wynne-Aherne *et al.* 1979). Other studies with a more selective method of assay are in progress. More recent examination of steady-state morphine pharmacokinetics using a radioimmunoassay (Grabinski *et al.* 1981) with an extraction procedure reveals wide interindividual variation in free morphine plasma levels and morphine plasmas level in the free conjugated ratio. Plasma levels are higher than would be predicted from known morphine kinetic data. Much of the currently available information on morphine pharmacokinetics is derived from data based on single-dose administration of morphine and is of doubtful relevance to repeated administration. It is also clear that there is no simple relationship between the morphine plasma level

at steady-state and the presence or absence of analgesia
(Walsh *et al.* 1981).

These data supports the value of oral administration of an
aqueous formulation of morphine to provide significant
plasma levels of free morphine, and underlines the necessity
for individualization of dosage.

The last hours

Many patients become somewhat drowsy and confused in
their last hours and medication commonly has to be given by
injection at this time. Although a few seem to require less
narcotic and may become relatively over-sedated, those who
develop terminal restlessness may have increased pain with
decreased ability to convey this to others and it is therefore
usually wise to give the intramuscular equivalent to the
previous oral doses on a regular basis. Some patients develop
jerking or twitching movements and although they may not
be aware of this, their visitors will be disturbed. Diazepam
5–10 mg added to the routine injection should give control.
Fluid may accumulate in the lungs during the last hours and
give rise to the 'death rattle'. If we prepare for this
comparatively common occurrence and prescribe ahead for
injections of hyoscine (Scopolamine) 0.4–0.6 mg together
with the opiate, an experienced nurse will detect the first
signs and this injection added as required will usually prevent
this distress for the family and to other patients. It is
important to explain the aims of our medication to the family
keeping its vigil.

Terminal, confused restlessness must be controlled with
adequate sedation, especially in home care (*see* p.51).

Which opiate?

Twycross was invited to test the clinical impression fairly
common in the UK that diamorphine (heroin) was the opiate
of choice (Saunders 1963) In a series of studies in St.

Christopher's Hospice a crossover trial between morphine and diamorphine (to which 699 patients entered and 146 achieved a crossover) showed that given regularly at individually optimized doses in an elixir with cocaine and a phenothiazine there was no clinically observable difference (Twycross 1977). As diamorphine is not available in most countries this was an important finding. The Hospice, which had previously used only diamorphine, changed its practice in 1977 and morphine is now prescribed for all oral narcotic medication, for up to 80 per cent of all doses given. Only a minority (28.28 per cent) of patients received doses above 20 mg morphine orally during 1979 (equivalent to 10 mg by injection) (Walsh *et al.* 1981). Because of its greater solubility, diamorphine is retained for subcutaneous and intramuscular injections. The dose is scaled down in the ratio oral morphine:injected diamorphine 3:1. The number of patients needing the larger doses and therefore larger volume is small and morphine would be an acceptable alternative for all but a small minority (oral to injected morphine 2:1).

Experience shows that when regularly administered oral morphine is used as the narcotic therapy of choice in this setting there will only infrequently be the need to broaden the armamentarium to include other strong analgesics. The only others of this group likely to be prescribed in St. Christopher's are phenazocine and dextromoramide. Phenazocine (Narphen) is given when a patient dislikes the morphine solution or prefers a tablet (5 mg are equivalent to 25 mg morphine). Dextromoramide (Palfium) is short acting and is sometimes used for the rapid relief of an exacerbation of pain (5 mg equivalent to 15 mg morphine). Methadone is rarely prescribed. There is no problem of cumulation with morphine or diamorphine but the fate and excretion of methadone is more complex (Vere 1978). Although it has been widely used for ambulant and fitter groups of patients, life-threatening cumulation may occur among the frail and elderly. See Table 2 for comparable doses.

TABLE 2 *Alternatives to morphine solution*

Name	Dose interval	Tablet	Morphine equivalent	Comment
Dextromoramide (Palfium)	2 hours	5 mg	15 mg (peak effect)	Too short acting for regular use, good for occasional "breakthrough pain"
Diamorphine (Heroin)	4 hours	Used in mixture	Diamorphine:morphine = 1:1.5	Identical in use to morphine
Dipipanone (Diconal)	4 hours	10 mg (with cyclizine 30 mg)	5 mg	Addition of cyclizine causes marked sedation, especially if 2–3 tablets required
Levorphanol (Dromoran)	6–8 hours	1.5 mg	8 mg	Useful strong analgesic
Methadone (Physeptone)	Very long	5 mg	7.5 mg (for single dose)	Accumulation occurs with regular administration
Morphine sulphate (MST–1 Continus)	12 hours	10 mg	Morphine 5 mg 4 hourly	Useful new preparation. 30 mg, 60 mg, and 100 mg tablets may later be available
Nepenthe undiluted	4 hours	1 ml	12 mg	Normally used in solution with aspirin
Oxycodone pectinate (Proladone) suppository	8 hours	30 mg suppository	15 mg 4 hourly	Excellent analgesic suppositories
Phenazocine (Narphen)	6–8 hours	5 mg	25 mg	Useful strong analgesic in tablet form. Usually start with $\frac{1}{2}$ tablet 6 hourly

Pethidine is a short-acting drug. Given by mouth it is not more effective than paracetamol.
Pentazocine (Fortral) has not been found useful.

The Brompton cocktail

Mixtures under this and other titles containing different amounts of one or more of the narcotic drugs are widely used; hospital staff often do not know what their own mixture contains and little discrimination is used. Melzack *et al.* (1979) compared a formula containing alcohol and cocaine to a simple aqueous solution of morphine in a double-blind study and like Twycross (1979) showed that cocaine in the mixture added no sustained effect. We conclude that morphine in water or chloroform water (the traditional English vehicle used to render mixtures more palatable) is as effective as the previously popular mixtures and that the latter should be discontinued in view of confusions concerning the strength of the narcotic dose. A solution is normally to be preferred to tablets, the dose can be titrated accurately to the patient's need and may be increased without enlarging the volume taken. A patient whose dose for pain control progresses from one to three or four tablets is reminded on each drug round of that increase.

Alcohol was omitted from the St. Christopher's mixture without a controlled trial but is used separately as it enhances normal social interchange for the patients in a way open to no other tranquilliser. Like other diversions, a drink shared with family or friends may act as a potent reliever of all forms of pain.

No one drug and no routine method is the whole answer to the control of terminal pain. Regular giving is not a panacea, it is a pattern into which other treatments and a general approach should be integrated. Success in pain control is easier to achieve when realistic goals are set. A patient needing opiates for pain relief should usually be sleeping well within the first day or two. It is possible, especially with bone pain, that pain on movement may be more difficult to abolish and with a few patients this may never be fully achieved if supplementary treatment with non-steroidal anti-inflammatory drugs, radiotherapy, or nerve blocks are not possible or successful. However, once nights are good and rest during the day is pain free, most of these patients will accept some change in their level of activity.

4 ADJUVANT THERAPY IN PAIN CONTROL

The control of pain in patients with terminal malignant disease does not include only the correct use of analgesics. Other drugs can also be given which may reduce the dose of analgesic required or possibly avoid its use completely. In the following section drugs used as adjuvant therapy are listed and their indications discussed.

Non-steroidal anti-inflammatory drugs

These are extremely effective agents in the treatment of bone pain and give relief in 60–70 per cent of patients. They presumably act because many secondary carcinomas produce prostaglandins which sensitize free nerve-endings. As in arthritis there is no general consensus as to the most effective drug; aspirin, indomethacin, phenylbutazone, and others are all used. The pain from some subcutaneous metastases can also be relieved by non-steroidal anti-inflammatory drugs.

Glucocorticosteroids

These are widely used in the control of many types of pain in the terminally ill patient. The common factor in such pain is that it is caused by pressure produced both by tumour and peri-tumour inflammatory oedema. Steroids have an anti-inflammatory effect, reduce the total size of 'tumour plus oedema', and thus diminish pain. The following are examples of steroid use.

Headaches due to raised intracranial pressure

Dexamethasone 16 mg daily is given. The full effect is usually apparent in a few days and the dose can then be gradually reduced until the lowest effective dose is found, often dexamethasone 4–6 mg daily.

Nerve compression pain

Examples are Pancoast's syndrome from involvement of the brachial plexus by a carcinoma at the apex of the lung and 'sciatica' from sacral or pelvic tumour involving sacral nerves. The level of pain in these cases is usually high and most patients require opiate analgesics. However, the effective dose of opiates can often be reduced by the addition of steroids, using dexamethasone 6 mg daily or prednisolone 40 mg daily. They should be stopped after a week if there is no response; if effective they should be slowly reduced to minimize side-effects.

Lymphoedema

Steroids are sometimes useful in the treatment of painful lymphoedema. They seem especially valuable in patients with grossly swollen legs due to pelvic malignancy. They are only rarely useful in lymphoedematous arms associated with breast cancer where the condition is more often of long duration with less local inflammatory reaction. The dose is the same as that used in nerve compression.

Visceral pain

Steroids are occasionally used with effect in painful hepato-megaly and other types of visceral pain. Prednisolone 15–30 mg daily is normally adequate.

Bone pain

Steroids are less effective than the non-steroidal anti-inflammatory drugs in the control of this type of pain, but are occasionally of value if the latter drugs are not tolerated or are not giving relief. The dose is the same as that used for visceral pain.

Antispasmodic drugs

These are useful in two situations:

1. Intestinal colic. A proportion of patients, mainly with ovarian or colon malignancies, develop subacute obstruction. This is characterized by abdominal distension, altered bowel habit (usually diarrhoea), and bouts of colicky pain. The colic can be controlled by an anti-diarrhoeal drug such as loperamide (Imodium) or diphenoxylate with atropine (Lomotil). The dose may be given as required if colic is only rarely present, three or four times daily if colic is frequent.

2. Bladder spasm. This may be caused by bladder tumour, infection, or an indwelling catheter. It can be treated with emepronium bromide (Ceteprin).

Antibiotics

Secondary infection is a fairly common cause of pain in patients with advanced malignant disease. Antibiotics are used for pain control in the following situations:

1. *Pleural pain.* It is difficult to tell if the typical stabbing pain of pleurisy is caused by malignant involvement of the pleura or by secondary infection. Antibiotics are therefore always used first; if they are not effective analgesic drugs may be required or an intercostal nerve block performed.

2. *Deep infections.* These not only cause pain but also an offensive discharge which can be very distressing to the patient and his family. Bacteriology is not often helpful as many different organisms are found and both anaerobes and aerobes are present. In practice a combination of metronidazole and amoxycillin has proved successful in reducing both pain and discharge; the single agent chloramphenicol may be substituted as it is effective against both aerobes and anaerobes.

3. *Superficial infections.* Antibiotics such as those used for deep infections are occasionally helpful, but more often local

measures are required (see Management of Fungating Growths, p. 48).

Tranquillizers

Major tranquillizers

These consist of the phenothiazines; e.g. chlorpromazine and prochlorperazine, and the butyrophenones, e.g. haloperidol. These have been traditionally prescribed in conjunction with opiate analgesics for three purposes: (i) to counteract opiate-induced nausea or vomiting; (ii) to potentiate the analgesic; and (iii) to tranquillize.

These points are considered in more detail below.

(i) There is now evidence to suggest that the emetic effect of opiates is not always present and that it ceases after a few days in the majority of cases. Some doctors will prefer to give morphine alone, only adding a phenothiazine or other antiemetic if vomiting occurs. This may be appropriate if the patient is under observation in hospital; for a less closely supervised patient at home it is probably best to introduce morphine with an antiemetic such as prochlorperazine (Stemetil) 5 mg 4 hourly or thrice daily and withdraw it later if possible.

(ii) Little is understood regarding the potentiation of opiates and further work in this field is required.

(iii) Anxiety undoubtedly increases the total experience of pain, so a very anxious patient should be prescribed a major or minor tranquillizer as well as being given full opportunity to talk over his fears with staff.

Minor tranquillizers

These include the benzodiazepines, e.g. diazepam and lorazepam. Many clinicians will be familiar with the rapid drop in analgesic requirement when a patient becomes less anxious, either due to the prescribing of an anxiolytic drug such as diazepam or more commonly the resolving of some emotional problem.

Antidepressants

The S.A.D. Index is a concept outlined by Black and Chapman (1976). They postulated that pain has three components—somatic injury, anxiety, and depression—increase in any of these increasing total experience of pain. This is borne out by the experience of many doctors in this field who have found that the prescribing of a trycyclic antidepressant drug for a clinically depressed patient may have an effect in lessening pain. Whether antidepressants have an analgesic effect in a non-depressed patient is not known, and results from current studies are awaited.

Tricyclic antidepressants are poorly tolerated in the terminally ill patient, and the starting dose should be low, usually 25 mg at night. This may be gradually increased to 75 mg at night but a higher dose, especially at first, often causes excessive drowsiness or confusion.

Monoamine oxidase inhibitors (MAOI) are best avoided in the terminal cancer patient as they may interact with other drugs he requires. On the other hand it is not justifiable to withold strong analgesia from a patient in severe pain who is, or has been, taking MAOI. Introduction of morphine should be done under observation, with regular blood pressure measurement and the starting dose should be very low.

With the analysis of causes of pain in cancer patients shown in page 17 and the adjuvant drugs discussed above it becomes possible to offer a rational treatment of cancer pain (Table 3). This combines the use of analgesic drugs and adjuvant therapy.

The ideal method of using such a table would be to apply the primary treatment for about a week in the hope that pain would be relieved or lessened and then only if necessary proceed to the secondary treatment. However, we know that patients often present with a long history of severe unrelieved pain and the only humane course then is to use all the available methods of relief, withdrawing ineffective treatment if and when possible.

TABLE 3 *Rational treatment of cancer pain*

Causes of pain	Primary treatment	Secondary treatment	Further treatment
Visceral from involvement of abdominal or pelvic organs	Analgesics	Low-dose steroids may help	Coeliac axis block for abdominal pain. Intrathecal block for pelvic pain
Bone pain	1. Palliative radiotherapy 2. Non-steroidal anti-inflammatory drugs 3. Immobilization e.g. cervical collar or pinning	Analgesics	Nerve block Low-dose steroids may help
Soft-tissue infiltration	Analgesics	Low-dose steroids and NSAIDs may help	Nerve block
Nerve compression	Analgesics	High-dose steroids	Nerve block
Secondary infection			
Deep	Systemic antibiotics including metronidazole if possibility of anaerobes. Local surgery.	Analgesics	Nerve block
Superficial	Systemic antibiotics. Local applications e.g. povidone-iodine		
Pleural pain	Antibiotics if appropriate	Analgesics	Intercostal block
Colic due to bowel obstruction	Faecal softeners. Antispasmodics, e.g. loperamide (Imodium)	Analgesics	
Lymphoedema	Analgesics. Intermittent positive pressure machine	High-dose steroids may help	Diuretics rarely of use
Headaches from raised intra-cranial pressure	High-dose steroids. Raise head of bed	Avoid opiate analgesics if possible	Diuretics may help
Pain in paralysed limb(s)	Physiotherapy and regular movement of limb(s) by nurses	Non-steroidal anti-inflammatory drugs	Muscle relaxants

5 CONTROL OF SYMPTOMS OTHER THAN PAIN

Nausea and vomiting

An attempt should be made to find the cause as specific treatment is available for some of the causes of vomiting in the terminally ill patient.

Hypercalcaemia

This should be suspected in patients with widespread bony metastases. Mild hypercalcaemia can be treated with glucorcorticosteroids, prednisolone 30 mg daily reducing as possible. More severe hypercalcaemia may require fluids and phosphate.

Raised intracranial pressure

Dexamethasone 16 mg daily, reducing slowly when possible.

Constipation—See page 45.

Drug induced

If it is not possible to withdraw the drug phenothiazines are usually effective. However, in many cases of vomiting no specific treatment is possible and antiemetics are required.

Phenothiazines

These include chlorpromazine (Largactil) and prochlorperazine (Stemetil). These are probably the most useful drugs, especially if vomiting is caused by biochemical changes. Chlorpromazine is used if sedation is also required. They are available as tablet, syrup, injection, and suppository. The following doses are suggested. Chlorpromazine: by mouth,

43

12.5–25 mg 4–8 hourly; injection, 25 mg 4–8 hourly; suppository, 100 mg 8 hourly. Prochlorperazine: by mouth, 5 mg 4–8 hourly; injections, 12.5 mg 8 hourly; suppository, 25 mg 8 hourly.

Metoclopramide (Maxolon)

This is particularly useful if vomiting is caused by delayed gastric emptying. It is available as tablet, syrup or injection, in each case 10 mg three times daily before meals.

Antihistamines

These include cyclizine (Valoid); this is useful in all types of vomiting, and is available as tablet or injection 50 mg three times daily. In some cases of intractable vomiting a combination of drugs from these different groups has proved effective when a single agent has failed.

Obstructive vomiting

This is fairly common in the later stages of abdominal malignancies, especially ovarian. It is usually of slow onset, at first intermittent.

A faecal softener such as ducosate (Dioctyl) should be given in the early phases with an antiperistaltic drug such as loperamide (Imodium) if required for painful colic. As the condition progresses the patient will require analgesics and antiemetics at first by mouth, later by injection or rectally. With their correct use it is possible to control both abdominal pain and persistent nausea so that the final phase need not be distressing.

Anorexia

This is very common in patients with widespread malignant disease. The only effective drug treatment is with steroids, prednisolone 15–30 mg daily. Alcohol before or with meals may help.

Dry or painful mouth

This may be due to candida, dehydration and anticholinergic drugs. Oral hygiene is of first importance and also early recognition of thrush with treatment of both mouth and dentures by nystatin oral suspension, 100 000 units in 1 ml four times daily.

Intravenous fluids and nasogastric feeding cannot be justified in dying patients. They rarely feel thirsty and it is perfectly possible to correct the only common symptom of dehydration, a dry mouth, by local measures such as frequent small drinks or crushed ice to suck and scrupulous attention to mouth care.

Hiccough

Either chlorpromazine (Largactil) 25 mg by mouth or i.m. or metoclopramide (Maxolon) 10 mg orally or i.m. may be effective.

Constipation

Most dying patients are constipated. This is due to a combination of factors; inactivity, anorexia, low-residue diet, and analgesic drugs.

It is best treated with a combination of softening and peristalsis-inducing aperients, conveniently given in a proprietary product such as Dorbanex medo or forte 5–10 ml twice daily (danthron and poloxamer). Normax (danthron and dioctyl) is similar, the dose being one or two capsules twice daily.

Suppositories or an enema or a manual removal may be needed if a patient presents with a loaded rectum or if the aperient regimen is not effective. A good general rule is for a rectal examination to be performed on the third day if the bowels have not opened and suppositories inserted if the rectum is loaded.

Diarrhoea

The causes of diarrhoea may be divided into:

1. Constipation with overflow. Treatment is with enema or suppositories followed by aperients.

2. Subacute obstruction. Use antiperistaltic drugs such as loperamide (Imodium) or diphenoxylate with atropine (Lomotil).

3. Malabsorption, usually from pancreatic insufficiency. Use pancreatic replacements, pancreatic tablets two or three with each meal (Pancrex, Pancrex V).

4. Rectal carcinoma. The diarrhoea will be accompanied by rectal discharge and the symptoms may be improved by prednisolone retention enemas, or foam or suppositories. These are also effective in the rectal discharge which occurs in patients who have had a palliative colostomy for rectal carcinoma.

5. Drug-induced diarrhoea and bowel infections need the usual treatment.

Dyspnoea

As in general medicine the cause should be found whenever possible and specific treatment instituted, e.g. diuretics in cardiac failure and bronchodilators in bronchospasm.

However, the following groups of drugs are of special interest.

Glucocorticosteroids

Superior vena caval obstruction can be treated with dexamethasone 8–12 mg daily either before radiotherapy or alone if this is inappropriate. The same dose will help in dyspnoea due to lymphangitis carcinomatosa. Reduce the dose when possible.

Dexamethasone 4–6 mg daily or prednisolone 30–40 mg daily is effective in bronchospasm.

Antibiotics

It is important to consider each case individually before embarking on treatment. Factors to consider are the symptoms caused by the chest infection, the patient's age and family ties, his general condition and respiratory capacity. If antibiotics are not given then symptoms present must be relieved with opiates and hyoscine.

Opiates

The mode of action in these drugs is uncertain, but they certainly relieve the sensation of dyspnoea.

Morphine 5–10 mg 4 hourly in a mixture or morphine sulphate (MST-1 Continus) may well be adequate, the dose should be titrated against the response, as with controlling pain and increased as necesary. A tranquillizing drug such as chlorpromazine (Largactil) or diazepam (Valium) may be added to combat associated anxiety.

With severe dyspnoea an injection of diamorphine 5–10 mg may be required.

Hyoscine

An injection of hyoscine 0.4–0.6 mg is given to dry up excessive secretions which accumulate when a patient is dying, so causing the 'death rattle'. The dose can be repeated 4–8 hourly if required. It should be given with an opiate, usually diamorphine 5–10 mg to increase sedation and prevent the occasional excitement caused by hyoscine.

Oxygen

This can be useful in acute dyspnoea, but infinitely better control of chronic dyspnoea can be obtained with the opiates.

Cough

Expectorants

Drugs such as ammonium chloride and ipecacuanha are

included in many 'expectorant' mixtures. They are not of proved efficacy. Patients benefit if they can stop smoking or inhale warm, moist air, e.g. Tincture of Benzoin inhalation.

Mucolytics

Bromhexine (Bisolvon) 8 mg three times daily is occasionally helpful in reducing the viscosity of bronchial secretions.

Suppressants

It is reasonable to suppress an unproductive cough expecially at night to allow rest. Codeine, pholcodeine, and methadone linctuses are used in ascending order of efficacy.

Urinary frequency and incontinence

These may be caused by urinary infections, polyuria from diabetes, constipation, neurological causes, and pelvic disease. Many of these respond to specific treatment. If treatment is not successful the following should be considered:

1. *Emepronium bromide (Cetiprin)*. This is useful in urinary frequency, especially nocturia; 100–200 mg three times daily or 200 mg at night.

2. *Condom*. This is useful for nocturnal incontinence but is not often tolerated throughout the 24 hours for long periods.

3. *Catheter*. This is usually the best way of treating severe frequency or incontinence as the risks of long-term catheterization no longer apply.

Fungating growths

Breast cancer is the commonest malignancy to cause fungation, but open lesions can also occur with other tumours.

1. Radiotherapy, cytotoxic drugs, and hormonal manipulation should be considered.

2. Regular cleansing is essential and an emulsion of 4%

povidone–iodine solution (Betadine) with liquid paraffin in a ratio of 1 : 4 has been found most effective. It is used to clean the wound, then gauze soaked in it is applied as a deodorizing and non-adhesive dressing.

3. For vulval lesions chlorhexidine gluconate (Hibitane) 1 in 2000 is used for frequent washdowns.

4. Gauze soaked in adrenalin 1 in 1000 may reduce capillary bleeding.

5. A course of an appropriate systemic antibiotic may help to reduce sepsis with its associated offensive discharge. The addition of metronidazole (Flagyl) should be considered if anaerobic infection is suspected.

Itch

1. In the irritation caused by biliary stasis cholestyramine (Questran) is the drug of choice, one sachet four times daily.

2. Antihistamines. Trimeprazine (Vallergan) 10 mg three times daily or promethazine (Phenergan) 25 mg at night.

3. Crotamiton (Eurax) and topical steroids are useful local antipruritic agents.

Insomnia

Hypnotics

Barbiturates and the long-acting benzodiazepines (nitrazepam and diazepam) are best avoided unless the patient requests them. The short-acting benzodiazepines are preferable as they do not cause cumulative sedation.

Temazepam (Normison) 10–30 mg at night is usually satisfactory.

Chlormethiazole (Heminevrin) is a good hypnotic for the elderly as it is most unlikely to precipitate or increase confusion. The usual dose is 1 g at settling, but a further 500 mg can be given with benefit in the early evening or if the patient is restless in the night.

Night sweats

These are an occasional cause of insomnia and often respond
to indomethacin 100 mg as required at night or Indocid-R
75 mg, a sustained-release preparation.

Night pain

This is a common cause of sleeplessness, especially in
paralysed patients who are unable to move and therefore
develop stiff joints and painful pressure areas. They benefit
from morphine 10 mg or morphine sulphate (MST-1
Continus) 10 mg at night.

Anxiety and depression

Psychotropic drugs play a minor role in the treatment of these
conditions. The two most important considerations are:
relief of physical symptoms; and emotional and spiritual
support for the patient and his family, with time given by
doctors, nurses, and social workers for full discussion of
problems (*see* p. 53).

The two useful groups of anxiolytic drugs are the
phenothiazines and benzodiazepines: individual patients
seem to do better on one than the other. Diazepam (Valium)
2–5 mg three times daily or chlorpromazine (Largactil)
10–25 mg three times daily can be used.

The value of tricyclic antidepressant drugs in a patient
facing death is difficult to determine and clinical depression
hard to separate from natural sadness. However, some
patients seem to benefit from tricyclics, especially those with
a protracted illness. The starting dose should be low:
amitriptyline (Tryptizol) 25 mg or imipramine (Tofranil)
25 mg at night, increasing slowly to 75 mg at night.

Confusion

The differential diagnosis of confusion in terminally ill
patients is a common and most difficult problem. However,

an attempt must be made at diagnosis as there are some specific treatments available: antibiotics for a chest infection, a reduction in sedative drugs and the use of glucocorticosteroids in cerebral metastases. Some persistently confused patients remain quiet and appear content; these should not be given psychotropic drugs. It is the restless, confused patient who is distressing to family and staff who needs sedation.

Haloperidol (Serenace) 5–10 mg i.m. is useful in an emergency, to be followed by the oral preparation 5–10 mg daily in divided doses.

Thioridazine (Melleril) 25 mg three times daily is suitable for the elderly; it does not cause much sedation.

Chlorpromazine (Largactil) 50–100 mg immediately followed by 25–50 mg three times daily is of use if extra sedation is required. Chlormethiazole (Heminevrin) has been mentioned as a good hypnotic for the elderly, without the risk of precipitating or increasing confusion.

Terminal restlessness

This may be due to unrelieved pain, or a distended bladder or rectum, but often no obvious cause is found. Probably the best drug in this situation is methotrimeprazine (Veractil or Nozinan), a very potent phenothiazine with analgesic properties. 50 mg should be given by injection with diamorphine if indicated; it can be repeated 4 hourly if necessary though usually 8 hourly is adequate.

Methotrimeprazine (Veractil) injections are still only obtainable by special order from the manufacturer, May and Baker. If they are not available chlorpromazine (Largactil) 50–100 mg 4–8 hourly can be substituted.

Diazepam (Valium) 5–10 mg i.m. is used in the last day or so to control muscle twitching and it can be combined with methotrimeprazine and diamorphine (though not in the same syringe) when restlessness is not controlled by these two drugs alone. The use of hyoscine for the 'death rattle' has already been mentioned (*see* p. 47).

Emergencies

These include major haemorrhage from any site, pulmonary embolus, a severe choking attack, and fracture of a large bone. The most rapid relief is given by the immediate injection of diamorphine 5–10 mg with hyoscine 0.4 mg. This combination often gives a retrograde amnesia for the event which may be of value if recovery occurs.

Convulsions

Some patients with cerebral tumours and uraemia develop fits. Prophylactic anticonvulsants are not usually given, but if a fit occurs the patient is started on sodium valproate (Epilim) 200 mg three times daily, increasing if necessary until fits are controlled or a satisfactory plasma level obtained. Phenytoin (Epanutin) 100 mg three times daily can be used similarly, but is less suitable in terminal care as it interacts with other drugs which may be needed.

When a patient is unable to take oral anticonvulsants he should be changed to i.m. phenobarbitone 60 mg twice daily. The depressing effect of the drug is no longer relevant and it is a convenient small injection.

Status epilepticus is rare; it should be treated with intravenous diazepam (Valium) given slowly at 10 mg/minute.

6 OTHER COMPONENTS OF 'TOTAL PAIN'

As we understand better the physical aspects of terminal care we find more subtle and complex problems to tackle. In the same way, as we face the totality of a patient's suffering we begin to understand more about its mental, social, and spiritual components and often find similar complexity. Where physical pain remains difficult to control these must be explored and although such division may be largely artificial it will enlighten us as we endeavour to understand a patient's suffering and to help him and his family.

The use of the word 'pain' must not trap us into thinking that it demands the immediate use of appropriate drugs. This pain should usually be faced rather than merely blotted out. There is often hard work to be done in this time of crisis and for some only the facing of the deepest issues in anguish will enable them to emerge as a greatly strengthened family. Much use for the future may be made of this time and as in many other situations of crisis it is surprising how quickly this may be achieved. There seems to be some kind of 'Doppler effect' in the process of time as we reach the end of our lives.

Mental pain

It is rare to find among the results of the investigations and examinations with which a patient's notes are filled any comment on his feelings or estimation of his insight into what is happening. These may well be his main problems and greatly exacerbate his total pain and undermine his capacity to cope with increasing weakness. Any illness causes anxiety, especially one that becomes more serious despite a variety of

53

treatments until it is patently life threatening. Patients tend to be left alone with these fears and receive only reassurances which they suspect are false. Mental suffering is likely to be enhanced by any physical distress; the doctor can do much to relieve the one as the other is tackled. Competent symptom control brings support at a deep level, demanding time with the patient and the close contact often denied at this stage; isolation adds to all suffering, particularly to the feeling of failure and the sense of guilt suffered by many dying patients. Here mental pain may be compounded by spiritual issues (*see* p. 62).

Only a minority of patients are likely to have a history of psychiatric or emotional disorder, but it is important to discover this at the first history taking. These patients may not need special help but difficulties will at least be easier to understand. Nearly all will be helped by a chance to talk of their feelings with a sympathetic listener, and while only a few will need the help of a psychiatrist, all of us can learn by discussing these reactions both with psychiatrists and with social workers. Their role is likely to be found more often in such consultations, meeting the patient at 'second hand', and in our experience ward meetings in which they are involved will encourage all the staff to develop their own confidence and expertise.

Those who have had the opportunity to listen constantly to dying people recognize a variety of reactions among them. Ross (1970) described these as stages of realization and Parkes (1978a) compared them with the progress through bereavement and other forms of loss. Both of these writers emphasize that some of these stages may be omitted, that they may not occur in clear-cut order, may overlap or may be gone through more than once, particularly in an illness that has remissions and relapses or a series of progressive deteriorations. Any attempt to impose a kind of blueprint would be wrong but many of us have seen our patients make a journey and we can expect progress and hope for adjustment to what is happening. Most human beings have the capacity for coming to terms with their circumstances which they retain even as death approaches, though for some it is a struggle that is deeply painful to watch.

Anyone who is faced with disaster or bad news tends to react initially with disbelief or denial. This is difficult to sustain and as it begins to waver a patient may display yearning and protest similar to the restless pining of early bereavement (Parkes 1972). They may feel angry about what is happening to them and project this on to their treatment and those who gave it to them, to their families and to fate: 'I was all right until I had radiotherapy'; 'The operation went wrong'; 'It's your pills, doctor'. Similar feelings are often present in the family who are facing bereavement, who may also defend themselves from its pain by projecting their anger on to the staff. These are feelings which can be worked through if they can be expressed to people who understand something of the reason for them and do not react by offended silence or withdrawal. It is at this point that the help of a social worker or psychiatrist as back-up to the ward team can be particularly helpful.

The next 'stage' is reached when a patient appears to give up hope, turns the anger on himself, and lapses into depression and despair. Such people only rarely contemplate suicide but those around often fear this and boost hope again, however unjustified this may be. This inhibits further progress towards adjustment. This phase is perhaps best regarded as sadness, a natural reaction, rather than as clinical depression. Used with discrimination antidepressant drugs sometimes help (*see* p. 50) but the listener who understands and is not overwhelmed by the situation helps most of all.

Many people can and do work their way through all these reactions. Hinton (1963) Parkes (1972) Ross (1970) and Weisman (1972) all describe a 'last stage' of acceptance and our experience would endorse this. People can come to accept death as inevitable although a faint hope of an unexpected recovery against all expectations may remain at the same time. Hope can exist in different forms all through such an illness, gradually changing in content. The small day-by-day hopes help the patient to accept the responsibility of living the life that remains to him. The quality of such living and the maturity of someone who has reached this acceptance is seen by many in this field as the most powerful argument against any deliberate shortening of life. So many emotional and interpersonal problems seem only to be solved at the very end.

There are no hard rules. Some fortunate people seem able to make this journey with simplicity and scarcely any of the anguish. Their sadness at parting is comforted by the love and friendship of those around and they continue to give back the same. Others go through the whole process in one or two intense sessions and then take each day as it comes, perhaps never discussing the matter again, like the man who said 'I've had it all out with my wife, now we can relax and talk about something else'.

Just as hope may continue in a different guise throughout an illness so too may fear. Fears of parting, of what will happen to dependants, of pain and weakness, and of failing to cope are all common among dying patients (Parkes 1978a). Although the complexity of the problems faced by many are daunting it need not make us feel helpless. Dying is not a psychiatric illness and does not usually call for specialized skills in counselling. Those who distance themselves, feeling they can bring nothing but a lack of comprehension do not realize that it is often their attempt to understand and not success in doing so that eases the patient's loneliness. Their own feelings of helplessness bring them to the patient at his level and here they can help with silence more than with words. The person who came nearest to helping the dying Ivan Illich as he struggled through his anguished queries about the meaning of his life was the peasant boy who willingly stayed physically near to him (Tolstoy 1887).

Nurses are usually closer to their patients than doctors and are likely to hear more of the questions and fears. Team consultations are essential if we are to reach helpful understanding. The social worker can listen in a unique way, for she is not involved with physical therapy and has been trained to act as the recipient of unacceptable feelings and projected angers. Negative feelings in this situation may be frighteningly strong and these are better expressed than buried only to appear in different guise, often affecting both family and staff. Time with physiotherapists offers more than the pleasure of assisted movement or even the joy of tackling the stairs again, with the consequent reward of the weekend home. It is well known that the interested ward orderly may hear more than anyone of matters which a patient is unable to share with the professionals who surround him. We must not forget that boredom may be a major component of mental pain and a good gossip, like other distractions, the best way to relieve it. Imaginative occupational therapy and any chance to be creative are healing to such feelings; so too may be the contact with the group in a department separate from the ward.

The psychotropic drugs may help in bringing the burden of his illness within a particular patient's compass and they are widely used. Their prescription has been discussed above (p. 50). The narcotic group of drugs are themselves powerful tranquillizers and some of their effectiveness stems from this fact. Most dying patients are likely to have a drug of the phenothiazine group prescribed although this should never happen automatically. The tricyclic group of drugs are used empirically, and less often. In St. Christopher's Hospice 16 per cent of all patients are prescribed a drug of this group but this figure rises to 39 per cent for those who remain as patients for more than 3 months. (Twycross and Wald 1976). The use of these drugs is currently being studied (Walsh 1982).

The distinction between mental and social pain may be hard to sustain—for much of a patient's fears concern his family. Some of those we care for will be loners but for a majority of them we must widen our concern to the family and close friends.

Social pain

When an illness has a foreseeable end it is still true that many families will come to grips with the situation and will wish to look after a dying relative at home as long as possible. Although the trend is for a higher proportion of cancer deaths to occur in hospital, prolongation of life by the newer treatments often means that much of this extra time is spent at home (Ford and Pincherle 1978). Only a minority will require heavy nursing for any length of time but there may be a prolonged period of emotional strain for patient and family alike. If they can be helped to handle this it may be an important time for them all for it enables the survivors to prepare for parting and to make some restitution for the failures of the past and the patient to complete his 'unfinished business' (Ross 1970). Old tensions may become acute but even at this stage, often because it *is* the final stage, reconciliation is not uncommon and many people make this a remarkably fruitful time. People in crisis often show an astonishing ability to resolve long-standing problems and even to handle new ones. The family, like the patient, have a journey to travel and much patience and support may be needed as they battle their way through.

Time spent with the family on admission or soon after the giving of a poor prognosis will help to establish or reaffirm trust and confidence. Explanations of the probable progress of the disease, of what can be done to control pain and other likely symptoms and some discussions of the actual process of dying will be needed. People have frightening images of dying and the increasing dependence and physical changes in some dying patients may serve to enhance them. Yet it has been shown in many settings that with competent care almost all patients will sink quietly into unconsciousness and die peacefully. Families are unlikely to know this unless we tell them and may live with unnecessary fears to worsen their sorrow and natural apprehension. Other practical reassurances may be needed—e.g. who to contact in a crisis; how much to expect of a visiting nurse, a home help or a night sitter; and what aids or supplementary benefits may be obtainable.

Children and adolescents should be involved. Attempts to 'protect' them are usually counter-productive and they are deeply hurt if they are excluded. They need explanations of the disease and its treatment that the parent is unlikely to be able to give as well as reassurances that cancer is not contagious nor hereditary. Discussions with whole families, including the children and often the patient have gradually become more common in St. Christopher's Hospice. A strengthened Social Work Department has facilitated this but a doctor or senior nurse who can give time for unlimited listening can handle many such situations given the support of the rest of the ward team. This may not be easy in either a busy practice or an acute ward and the growth of specialized hospital or home care teams who will work alongside regular staff can bring extra time and experience where the latter are hard pressed.

The patient who is kept in the dark about family finances and various practical matters will have the added burden of fancying he has hurt or offended others because of the barriers thus erected. Financial burdens are often heavy, especially for those who have prolonged time off work, but the patient should be included in all discussion and plans as he should be involved as far as possible in ordinary family life. One can understand the strong desire to keep all worries from the patient, yet this protectiveness often leads to crippling tensions and it is sad since the patient is likely to come to know the truth by other means. To keep an unshared secret from an intimate inevitably impairs communication and can add greatly to the general distress: 'The successful open sharing of their stress which comes about spontaneously in some marital relationships has a quality which leads one to hope that more could be helped by a similar achievement' (Hinton 1970). Recent work by Stedeford (1981) has confirmed this.

We have also found that many couples are greatly relieved when they are encouraged slowly to share as much of the truth as they seem able to handle. Family relationships are often complex and disturbed but although some will demand much help from a social worker it is surprising how many will battle their own way through with the care and support of their usual doctors and nurses. A recent short paper has given some helpful guidelines (Earnshaw-Smith 1981).

If admission to hospital or hospice becomes necessary, it may bring comfort for the patient and reduction of anxiety for the family but these must not be brought at the cost of feelings of guilt. The family must be reassured that they have done what they could and that professional help is now needed on a full-time basis. The ward staff must not take over care in such a way as to exclude the family, who may not easily be involved with the physical care of the patient. When possible this should be encouraged but they can contribute greatly to his security and peace by their mere presence and this should certainly be made both possible and explicit. They are present as of right at this time, both cared for and caring and their unique role must be emphasized and reinforced. The social worker and the chaplain may still be much involved with those who react aggressively to their pain or are overwhelmed by their feelings but every member of staff should be able to give some recognition, even though brief, to the family that is maintaining its last watch with a dying member.

The long pain of the family's bereavement is a part of terminal pain. They will begin to grieve their imminent parting during the illness but the real letting go and approach to the new situation will rarely happen before the patient dies. The final watch and the witnessing of a peaceful death may be very important for some families; others cannot remain by the bedside. Staying there may not be possible or advisable and care must be taken to protect them from feelings of guilt and responsibility. Ward staff are all too familiar with the desolation of the final moment of parting and the empty numbness that follows it but do not always appreciate how greatly their supporting presence can help, both then and when the family returns afterwards.

An increasing number of units and teams in The Hospice Movement have included bereavement follow-up work and some have attempted to identify those families who appear to need extra support in the initial stages of their life without the patient (Parkes 1979). More work needs to be done in this field both in selecting those who need help and in understanding how best to give it. The social worker may well be in contact with such a family before the patient dies but the ward team should report unusually disturbed or disturbing behaviour. Some people from cultures different from our own may show noisy expressions of grief which must somehow be allowed without upsetting an entire ward. An inability to show any emotion is usually a poor prognostic sign.

Some families ask for sedatives but this is probably mistaken. Grief needs to be expressed at this point and drugs may inhibit this natural and eventually healing reaction. There is no ground for prescribing tranquillizers or antidepressants to the bereaved as a routine. Parkes (1978a) believes that such drugs should be reserved for the potentially suicidal, for whom a referral to expert help may be needed in an emergency. Such drugs may be needed by those who, despite all efforts to help, remain in a state of chronic agitation or depression. A mild hypnotic may be needed for those whose sleep remains disturbed.

The bereaved family comes slowly to full realization of

what has happened and after often intense inner struggle and dejection is eventually ready to build a new life. This may take many months and is felt like a sort of illness which is finally healed. Abnormal, unresolved grief needs skilled help.

The whole process of bereavement is not often seen by clinicians other than family doctors but all of us should accept two responsibilities. Firstly, to see that others are alert to identifying and helping those who are especially at risk in their loss; and secondly, to do all that is possible to ease the memories of those who live on by giving the best possible relief of terminal distress.

Most dying people show remarkable endurance and those who spend their time close to them find that this helps to reduce their own fears of death. The dying have a good heritage to leave which is not always recognized or received either by the staff around or, more important, by the family themselves. The bereaved too have much to hand on. Parkes writes of his admiration for many of the people who have shared their grief with him and finds that counselling them has made it easier to recognize bereavement as an acceptable part of life (Parkes 1978a).

Spiritual pain

Few people today are likely to express their doubts and griefs in terms that are recognizably religious. Nevertheless, feelings of failure and regret—'If only . . .'; 'I wish I hadn't . . .'; 'It's too late.'—are common and often intense. Many patients need help to face feelings of guilt that can truly be described as spiritual pain, sometimes amounting to deep anguish. This becomes apparent as we listen, however much the spiritual component may seem to be swamped by difficulties of personality, culture or past history. Some have a background of a 'Church' affiliation and early liaison with or through the chaplain in hospital or with the priest or minister of the patient's own choice at home may be important. His ability to pronounce the forgiveness that always awaits every man can be manifestly healing. Others have no such starting place but we have seen how an atmosphere of acceptance created by a whole ward team or by an individual member visiting in a home can reach and assuage such pain.

Our own religious convictions can help in creating such a climate but it is no precondition of effective help that a patient should accept these beliefs and each one must be so free of any pressure to conform that the thought never enters his mind. There is a progression from trust in the acceptance by others of all the things in ourselves that we regret into a faith in forgiveness, where we at last believe that they have no more power to hurt us or anyone else. We cannot change what has happened or what we have done, but we can come to believe that the meaning of the past can be changed. From this comes the ability to forgive ourselves. This may never be expressed in words on either side but the quality of the ensuing peace is unmistakable.

A feeling of meaninglessness, that neither oneself nor the universe itself has permanence or purpose, is a form of spiritual pain. Patients need to look back over the story of their lives and believe that there was some sense in them and also to reach out towards something greater than themselves, a truth to which they can be committed. This is often linked with the belief that somehow life goes on: 'In all of us the archaic belief in the immortality of the soul is still dormant' (Eissler 1955); 'As anyone who has done much pastoral or counselling work will know, the belief (or perhaps it would often be better described as a feeling or intuition) that our visible, physical life is not the whole of our personal history is exceptionally tenacious' (Baker 1981). The first writer was sure that this 'magic' belief, although it had no place in his scientific frame of reference, was present in both the patient and himself and should be used to help lift the burden of grief until the patient finally lost consciousness. The second, holding the conviction that 'God can and will re-create our being even beyond annihiliation', looked beyond to another dimension where the individual's capacity to love and worship will be fulfilled in freedom. We meet some who seem to have had little chance of a worthwhile life *or* death and find that our belief in a God who has himself gone through the rejection and death of a world of random pain and catastrophe keeps us close to such people with trust and hope for them.

Those hospices and homes that have some form of religious foundation will never care for more than a minority of all dying patients. Most will continue to die in their own homes or hospital wards where awareness of these issues is not normally seen as part of the care of the team as a whole. Here the ward sister is likely to be the person with whom the chaplain has most to do but some contact with a doctor may be essential. Consultation concerning the patient's needs and some idea of prognosis is required rather than detailed medical information and this is likely to be most effective when it is informal and continuing. It would be unwarranted intrusion to suggest a contact when there is no understanding nor willingness on the part of a patient and his family but a chaplain who makes himself informally available is often surprised at his welcome. The gap that exists between the ordained ministry and the rest of us is not as wide as many believe it to be.

But we cannot leave it all to the chaplain, who in any case is often greatly overworked. Whoever we are and whatever our beliefs we may have to face questions from the families and the patients and have to find the strength to listen when we feel we have no answers to give. The command 'Watch with me' did not mean 'Take this crisis away'; it could not have meant 'Explain it'; the simple, yet costly demand was 'Stay there and stay awake'. More of those who try to do this than will perhaps care to admit it will find themselves trusting in a Presence that can more easily reach the patient and his family if they themselves concentrate on using all their competence with compassion and say little to interrupt.

Staff pain

The staff themselves often need supporting, especially during their first weeks in terminal care. This work causes pain and bewilderment at times to all in this field and the closer the staff are to the weakness of the patients and the grief of the families the more they too will suffer the pangs of bereavement.

Nurses meeting death for the first time find it awe inspiring, even uncanny, and they and their colleagues in general wards are likely to question whether they did everything they should have done. They often feel overwhelmed and need an early opportunity to discuss this with someone more senior, preferably someone who has also known the patient. Those who choose to work in hospices are far more likely now than even 10 years ago to have had this opportunity during their general training and to have seen enough of what can be achieved in an acute ward to want to learn and then develop this in their turn.

Doctors are not immune to such feelings and are perhaps even more likely to question whether in fact the death was not due to a failure on their part. They may have had opportunity for discussion as students but even so the first death once they have qualified and have some responsibility may be unexpectedly traumatic.

Staff members of all disciplines may find themselves suffering a process of loneliness and exhaustion, protest, anger and depression and will need to share this if they are to find their way through. Merely to deny or repress such feelings hinders any progress to dealing with themselves and hence better with others in the future. The resilience of those who choose and continue to work exclusively in this field is won by a full understanding of what is happening and not by a retreat behind a technique. The initial impact of hospice work at first hand and the draining effect of its continual losses calls for some form of team or group support. This may well need to be varied; a series of group discussions seems to have a natural term and later another approach is needed. Spontaneous meetings that arise among those closely involved as a team continue to offer the most reliable as well as the most prompt and pertinent support.

Efficiency is always comforting. The giving of effective relief to all types of pain makes this an extremely rewarding field and in itself is a major form of support. Nevertheless, if we are to remain for long near the suffering of dependence and parting we need also to develop a basic philosophy and search, often painfully, for meaning in even the most adverse situations. We may be working with long and sometimes distressing physical retreats but these are so often more than balanced by emotional and spiritual advances. It is not to idealize to say that achievements are constantly being made during this time. From the dying themselves we learn not only to understand something of the ending of life but also a great deal to make us optimistic about all life and about the potential of those ordinary human beings who work their way through it.

We have to gain enough confidence in what we are doing and enough freedom from our anxieties to listen to another's distress. Only if we are prepared to do this will we find that most rewarding of all the aspects of terminal treatment and care: we will come continually to know people at their most mature, their most courageous.

REFERENCES

Aitken-Swan, J. and Easson, E. C. (1959). Reactions of cancer patients on being told their diagnosis. *Brit. Med. J.* **i**, 779.

Annals of Internal Medicine (1980). Ethical dilemmas and the clinician. *Annls. Intern. Med.* **92**, 116.

Baker, J. A. (1981). A philosophy for dying. In *Hospice—The living idea* (eds. C. M. Saunders, D. Summers, and N. Teller) p. 68. Edward Arnold, London.

Bates, T. (1978). In *Radiotherapy in terminal care in the management of terminal disease* (ed. C. M. Saunders) p. 119. Edward Arnold, London.

Beecher, H. K. (1960). *Quantitive effect of drugs.* Harvard University, London and New York; Oxford University Press.

Black, R. G. and Chapman, C. R. (1976). SAD Index for clinical assessment of pain. In *Advances in pain research and therapy* (eds. J. J. Bonica and A. Fessard) Vol. 1, p. 301. Raven Press, New York.

Brewin, T. B. (1977). The cancer patient: communication and morale. *Brit. Med. J.* **ii**, 1623.

Church Information Office (1975). *On dying well—An Anglican contribution to the debate on euthanasia.*

Council of Europe (1976). *Recommendation 779 on the Rights of the sick and dying.* 27th Ordinary Session, January.

Earnshaw-Smith, E. (1981). Dealing with dying patients and their relatives. *Brit. Med. J.* **282**, 1779.

Eissler, K. R. (1955). *The Psychiatrist and the dying patient.* p. 142. International Universities Press, New York.

Ford, G. R. and Pincherle, G. (1978). Arrangements for terminal care in the N.H.S. (especially those for cancer patients). *Hlth. Trends* **10**, 73.

Grabinski, P. Y., Kaiko, R. F., Walsh, T. D., Foley, K. M. and Houde, R. W. (1981). Morphine radioimmunoassay specificity before and after extraction of plasma and after extraction of plasma and cerebrospinal fluid. In press.

Graeme, P. (1961). The terminal care of the cancer patient. 1. The doctor. *St. Mary's Hosp. Gaz.* **67**, 118.

Greer, S., Morris, T., and Pettingale, K. W. (1979). Psychological Response to breast cancer: effect and outcome. *Lancet* **ii**, 785.

Hansard (1976). *Incurable patients bill.* Vol. 368, No. 31.

Hinton, J. (1963). Mental and physical distress in the dying. *Q. J. Med.* **32**, 1.

—— (1970). Communication between husband and wife in terminal cancer. Presented at the *Second international conference on social science and medicine*, 7–11 September, Aberdeen.

—— (1979). Comparison of places and policies for terminal care. *Lancet* **i**, 29.

Holden, T. (1980). Patiently speaking. *Nursing Times* June, 12, 1035.

Holford, J. M. (1973). *Terminal care. Care of the dying. Proceedings of a National Symposium held on 29 November 1972.* HMSO, London.

Hunt, J. M., Stollar, T. D., Littlejohns, D. W., Twycross, R. G., and Vere, D. W. (1977). Patients with protracted pain: A survey conducted at The London Hospital. *J. Med. Ethics* **3**, 61.

Journal of Medical Ethics (1981). *J. Med. Ethics* **7**, 56.

Kennedy, I. McC. (1978). The law relating to the treatment of the terminally ill. In *The of management of terminal disease* (ed. C. M. Saunders) p. 189. Edward Arnold, London.

Kubler-Ross, E. (1970). *On death and dying.* Tavistock Publications, London.

Lancet (1980). In cancer, honesty is here to stay. *Lancet* **ii**, 245.

Lamerton, R. (1979). Cancer patients dying at home: the last 24 hours. *The Practitioner* **223**, 813.

McIntosh, J. (1978). *Communication and awareness in a cancer ward.* Croom Helm, London.

Melzack, R., Mount, B. M., and Gordon, J. M. (1979). The Brompton mixture versus morphine solution given orally: effects on pain. *Can. Med. J.* **120**, 435.

Parkes, C. M. (1972). *Bereavement studies of grief in adult life.* Tavistock and Pelican, London.

—— (1978a). Psychological aspects. In *The management of terminal disease* (ed. C. M. Saunders). Edward Arnold, London.

—— (1978b). Home or hospital? Patterns of care for the terminally ill cancer patient as seen by surviving spouses. *J. R. Coll. gen. Prac.* **28**, 19.

—— (1979). Terminal care: evaluation of in-patient service at St. Christopher's Hospice. Part 1. Views of surviving spouse on effects of the service on the patient. *Postgrad. Med. J.* **55**, 517.

Parkes, C. M. and Parkes, J. L. N. (1982). Hospice versus hospital care: re-evaluation of ten years of progress in terminal care as seen by surviving spouses. Awaiting publication.

Pius, XII, Pope (1957). *Acta Apostolicae Sedia* **49**, 1027.

Rex *v.* Bodkin Admas (1957). Criminal Law Review.

Saunders, C. M. (1963). The treatment of intractable pain in terminal cancer. *Proc. R. soc. Med.* **56**, 195.

Stedeford, A. (1981). Couples facing death II—Unsatisfactory communication. *Brit. Med J.* **283**, 1098.

Suicide Act (1961). Section 2.

Tolstoy, L. (1887). *Ivan Ilych.* Oxford University Press.

Twycross, R. G. (1977). Choice of strong analgesia in terminal cancer: diamorphine or morphine? *J. Int. Assoc. study Pain* **3**, 93.

—— (1978). Relief of pain. In *The management of terminal disease* (ed. C. M. Saunders) p. 65. Edward Arnold, London.

—— (1979). Effect of cocaine in the Brompton cocktail. In *Advances in pain research and therapy* (eds. J. J. Bonica and D. Alke-Fessand) Vol. 3, p. 927. Raven Press, New York.

—— and Wald, S. J. (1976). Long term use of diamorphine in advanced cancer. In *Advances in pain research and therapy* (eds. J. J. Bonica and D. Alke-Fessand) Vol. 1, p. 653. Raven Press, New York.

—— Fry, D. E., and Wills, P. D. (1974). *Brit. J. Clin. Pharmacol.* **1**, 491.

Vanderpool, H. Y. (1978). The ethics of terminal care. *J. Am. med. Assoc.* **239**, 850.

Vere, D. W. (1978). *Topics in therapeutics 4.* Pitman, London.

Wall, P. D. (1979). On the relation of injury to pain. The John J. Bonica Lecture. *Pain* **6**, 253.

Walsh, T. D. (1980). Therapeutics in advanced cancer—research findings. In *Hospice—the living idea* (eds. C. M. Saunders, D. Summers, and N. Teller) p. 101. Edward Arnold, London.

—— (1982). In preparation.

—— Baxter, R., Bowman, K., and Leber, B. (1981). High dose morphine and respiratory function in chronic cancer pain. *Pain* **1**, 5–39.

—— and Bowman, K. (1981). Incidence and severity of depression in advanced cancer. In *Proceedings of the Third World Congress of Biological Psychiatry* Vol. 2, F507.

—— Moon, P., Spinks, M., Bowman, P., and Leber, B. (1981). Advanced cancer pain—Use of oral morphine. Abstract of talk given at the *UICC conference on clinical oncology*, Lausanne, October 1981.

Weisman, A. D. (1972). *On dying and denying—A psychiatric study of terminality.* Behavioural Publications, New York.

West, T. W. and Kirkham, S. R. (1980). Communication with patients and families. In *Hospice—the living idea* (eds. C. M. Saunders, D. Summers, and N. Teller). p.53. Edward Arnold, London.

World Health Organization. (1946). Constitution. WHO, Geneva.

Woodbine, G. (1977). *The care of patients dying from cancer, a cross-sectional study.* (Excerpt from M.Sc. Thesis.)

Wynne Aherne, G., Piall, E., and Twycross, R. G. (1979). Serum morphine concentration after oral administration of diamorphine hydrochloride and morphine sulphate. *Brit. J. clin. Pharmacol.* **8**, 577.

INDEX

71